THIS BOOK BELONGS TO:

....

IT WAS GIVEN TO ME BY:

....

ON THIS DATE:

....

PAJAMA PRAYERS

JEAN FISCHER

BEDTIME INSPIRATION FOR KIDS

BARBOUR kidz
A Division of Barbour Publishing

ISBN 979-8-89151-191-0

Cover and interior art: Camila Carrossine

Published by Barbour Publishing, Inc., 1810 Barbour Drive, Uhrichsville, Ohio 44683, www.barbourbooks.com

Our mission is to inspire the world with the life-changing message of the Bible.

Printed in China.
002642 0925 HA

TO MY MOTHER,
WHO TAUGHT ME TO PRAY.

THROUGH [GOD'S]
SHINING-GREATNESS
AND PERFECT LIFE,
HE HAS GIVEN US PROMISES.
THESE PROMISES ARE
OF GREAT WORTH
AND NO AMOUNT OF
MONEY CAN BUY THEM.

2 PETER 1:4

CONTENTS

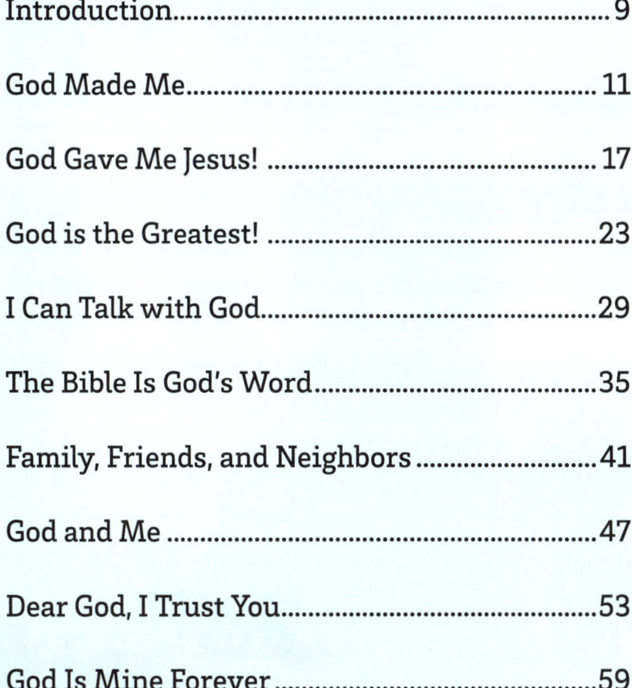

INTRODUCTION

EVERYTHING IN THE BIBLE IS TRUE

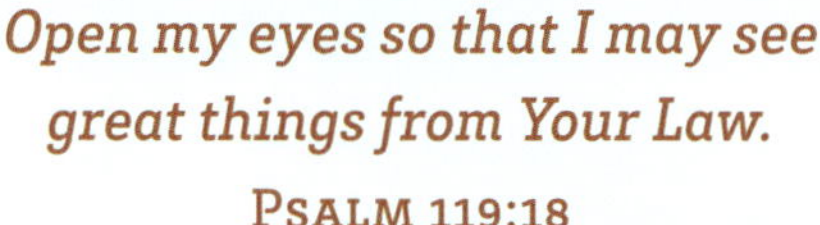

Open my eyes so that I may see great things from Your Law.

PSALM 119:18

Dear God, thank You for the Bible. It is filled with stories about how You help the people who love You. The Bible's words remind me that You love me and will help me every day, wherever I am. Best of all, the Bible is filled with promises that are for me—right now. So teach me about Your promises, God. I want to learn about them and live my life trusting in each one. Amen.

THINK ABOUT IT!

Why is it important to read the Bible?

GOD MADE ME

GOD CREATED ME

"Before I started to put you together in your mother, I knew you. Before you were born, I set you apart as holy. I chose you to speak to the nations for Me."

JEREMIAH 1:5

Dear God, help me to remember that You made me. Before I was born, even before You put my body together, You knew all about me. You planned what I would look like, where I would live, and all the people I would ever meet. You knew my favorite colors and what I would be really good at. Best of all, God, You made me to be Yours, always and forever. Thank You! Amen.

THINK ABOUT IT!

What do you like best about the way God created you?

I AM A GIFT FROM GOD

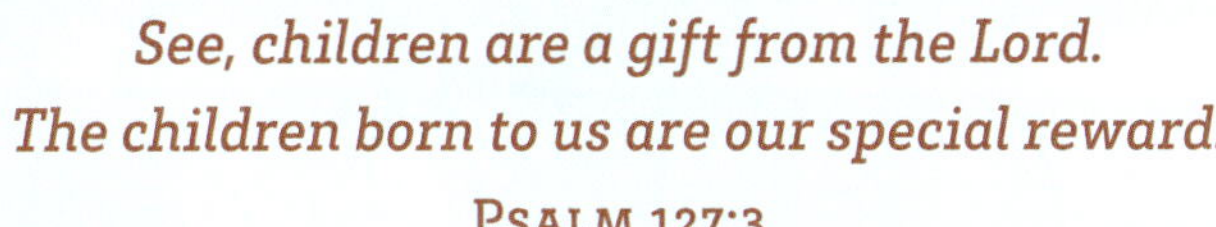

See, children are a gift from the Lord.
The children born to us are our special reward.

PSALM 127:3

Dear God, I've never thought of myself as a gift, but You say that's what I am. A gift is something special because it is given with love. When You created me, You made me special. You formed my body exactly the way You wanted it to be. Then You put all Your love into me and gave me to my parents. I am their best gift ever! I love You, God. Amen.

THINK ABOUT IT!

What makes you special?

GOD CHOSE ME

"The Lord your God has chosen you out of all the nations on the earth, to be His own."
DEUTERONOMY 7:6

Dear God, I feel special when someone chooses me as a friend, and I feel extra special knowing that You chose me to be Yours. You made me so You could love me now and forever. You created me as one of a kind. In the whole world, there is no one just like me. Tonight when I close my eyes to sleep, I will remember that You chose me to be Your own. Good night, God. Amen.

THINK ABOUT IT!

In what ways are you different (and special!) from everyone else?

GOD MADE ME BEAUTIFUL

"You are all beautiful, my love. You are perfect."

SONG OF SOLOMON 4:7

Dear God, everything You make is perfect, and that is how You made me. I am Your perfect creation. You made me the way You wanted me to be. And when You finished making me, You looked at me and decided that I was the most beautiful child You had ever seen. You feel that way about me all the time. So help me to remember every day that I am Your beautiful child. Amen.

THINK ABOUT IT!

What is your favorite thing about God's creation?

GOD GAVE ME A BEAUTIFUL HEART

Your beauty should come from the inside. It should come from the heart. This is the kind that lasts. Your beauty should be a gentle and quiet spirit. In God's sight this is of great worth and no amount of money can buy it.

1 PETER 3:4

Dear God, when You created me, You gave special attention to my heart. You made it a beautiful place that You can fill with Your love. You have poured so much love in there that I have plenty left over to share with others. Thank You, dear God, for my beautiful heart! I love You so much. Amen.

THINK ABOUT IT!

What makes someone's heart beautiful?

GOD GAVE ME JESUS!

GOD SENT US JESUS

"For God so loved the world that He gave His only Son. Whoever puts his trust in God's Son will not be lost but will have life that lasts forever."

JOHN 3:16

Dear God, sometimes it is hard for people to do what is right. You knew that, so You sent Your Son, Jesus, to help us. You sent Jesus to teach us to be right and good. You sent Him to be with us all the time, now and forever. Best of all, Jesus will lead us to heaven someday. Thank You, God, for giving us Jesus. He is the best gift of all. Amen.

THINK ABOUT IT!

Why is Jesus the best gift?

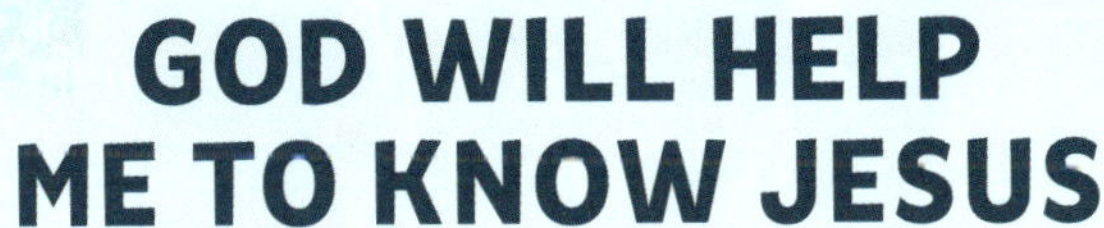

GOD WILL HELP ME TO KNOW JESUS

Learn to know our Lord Jesus Christ better. He is the One Who saves.

2 PETER 3:18

Dear God, I want to know all about Jesus. Open my heart to let Him in. Teach me about Him through the Bible and wherever I go—at home, school, church, and play. I know that Jesus is real. He is my friend. Jesus is with me all the time, and I can depend on Him. I want to trust Jesus and become more like Him every day. Please help me to know Him better. Amen.

THINK ABOUT IT!

In what ways do you depend on Jesus?
Is He your very best friend?

JESUS WANTS TO LIVE WITH ME

"See! I stand at the door and knock. If anyone hears My voice and opens the door, I will come in to him."

REVELATION 3:20

Dear Jesus, I want You to live in my heart so You can be with me forever. I can imagine my heart is like a house with a door. I can think of You knocking on the door and calling my name. All I have to do is open the door and invite You inside. Will You come into my heart right now, Lord Jesus? I want You to live with me now and forever. Amen.

THINK ABOUT IT!

Is Jesus in your heart?

JESUS LOVES CHILDREN

He took the children in His arms. He put His hands on them and prayed that good would come to them.

MARK 10:16

Dear Jesus, You love kids. I know because the Bible says so. When You lived here on earth, You wanted the children to come to You. You held them in Your arms, and You prayed for them. Today, You live in the hearts of everyone who believes in You. It makes me happy knowing that You live in my heart and that You will help with whatever I do. I love You, Jesus! Amen.

THINK ABOUT IT!

How does it feel to know that Jesus loves kids?

JESUS HELPS ME WITH EVERYTHING

I can do all things because
Christ gives me the strength.
PHILIPPIANS 4:13

Dear Jesus, You are my helper. You help me be strong whenever I feel weak. When I think that I can't do something, You help me to try anyway. If I fail, You help me to try again. When something is difficult and I want to give up, You give me strength to keep on going. I am never alone, Jesus, because You are always with me and helping me. Thank You so much! Amen.

THINK ABOUT IT!

In what ways has Jesus helped you get through something hard?

GOD IS THE GREATEST!

GOD'S PROMISES NEVER FAIL

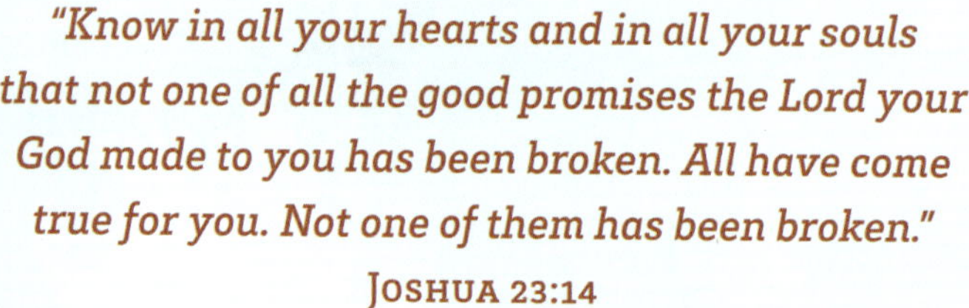

"Know in all your hearts and in all your souls that not one of all the good promises the Lord your God made to you has been broken. All have come true for you. Not one of them has been broken."

JOSHUA 23:14

Dear God, I love learning about Your promises. I am finding out that the Bible is filled with them, and all of them are good. Every one of Your promises is true and perfect. One of the best things about You is that You are always trustworthy. I know that when You make a promise, You will keep it. God, help me to be more like You. I want to keep my promises too. Amen.

THINK ABOUT IT!

How many promises does God keep—
just a few. . .or ALL of them?

GOD IS THE GREAT, FOREVER KING

We give honor and thanks to the King Who lives forever. He is the One Who never dies and Who is never seen. He is the One Who knows all things. He is the only God. Let it be so.

1 TIMOTHY 1:17

Dear God, the Bible says that You are the King of everything. I can't see You, but You are all around me ruling the world. It says that You will live forever and that You know everything. No human king is like You or could ever do what You do. That's because You are God—the one and only God. Thank You for watching over me, knowing all about me, and loving me so much. Amen.

THINK ABOUT IT!

If God knows "everything," what kinds of things does He know?

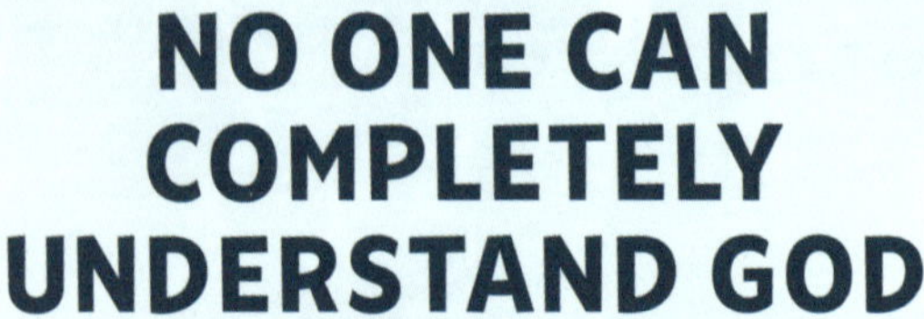

NO ONE CAN COMPLETELY UNDERSTAND GOD

God's riches are so great! The things He knows and His wisdom are so deep! No one can understand His thoughts. No one can understand His ways.

ROMANS 11:33

Dear God, I have so many questions about You. Why can't I see You? What do You look like? How can You know everything about everybody all the time? Some things about You are just too great for humans to understand. I believe that You love me and that You will always take care of me. Help me to trust You even when there is so much that I don't understand. Good night, God. I love You. Amen.

THINK ABOUT IT!

What kinds of questions would you ask God if you could talk to Him face-to-face?

GOD IS EVERYWHERE

He is the One Who makes the mountains and the wind. He makes His thoughts known to man. He turns the morning into darkness, and walks on the high places of the earth. The Lord God of All is His name.

AMOS 4:13

Dear God, the earth is so big. Still, You are everywhere right now. You are with me and also with every other child in the world—You are with everyone. You are in the fields, forests, deserts, jungles, and even in places that are frozen and cold. You are up in the sky among the stars and the clouds and in the deepest oceans. How do You do that, God? I think You are amazing. Amen.

THINK ABOUT IT!

Where is God?

GOD KNOWS EVERYTHING

"For My thoughts are not your thoughts, and My ways are not your ways," says the Lord. "For as the heavens are higher than the earth, so are My ways higher than your ways, and My thoughts than your thoughts."

Isaiah 55:8–9

Dear God, I want to remember that You always do what is best for me. You know everything that goes on with me and what I am thinking. You might not always agree with what I want. That is because Your plans for me are better than my own plans. You know exactly what I need. So, if something doesn't go my way and I feel disappointed, please remind me that You know best. Amen.

THINK ABOUT IT!

Why are God's plans always best?

I CAN TALK WITH GOD

GOD WANTS ME TO TALK WITH HIM

Never stop praying.

1 THESSALONIANS 5:17

Dear God, before I go to sleep, I want to thank You for prayers. Praying is how I can talk with You. Since You are with me all the time, I know that I can talk with You wherever I am. I can ask You about anything and tell You about my thoughts and feelings. Whatever I need, I can ask You for it. Thank You for prayers, God, and for listening to me tonight. Amen.

THINK ABOUT IT!

Does God really hear every prayer?

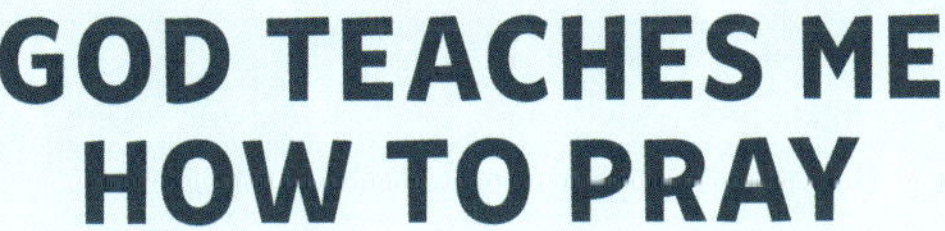

GOD TEACHES ME HOW TO PRAY

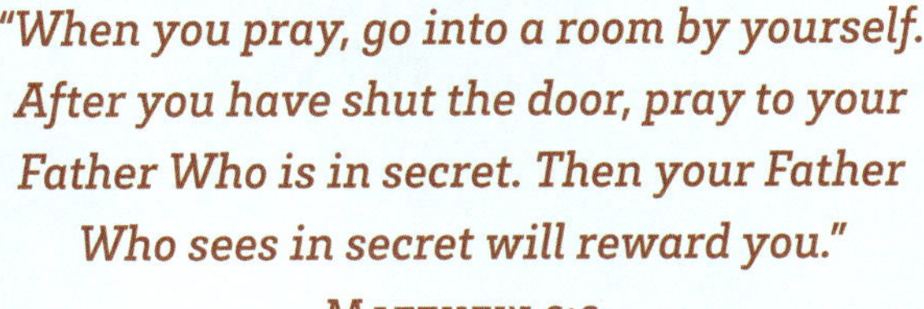

"When you pray, go into a room by yourself. After you have shut the door, pray to your Father Who is in secret. Then your Father Who sees in secret will reward you."

MATTHEW 6:6

Dear God, please help me to set aside some quiet time each day to talk with You. Teach me to pray about everything and ask for whatever I need. Show me that I don't have to use special words when I pray. I can talk with You all the time as if I am talking with my closest friend—because that is who You are, my very best friend. I love You, God. Amen.

THINK ABOUT IT!

Where is your favorite place to talk to God?

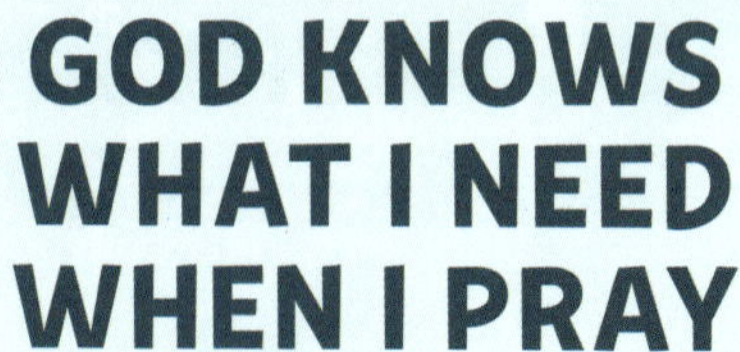

GOD KNOWS WHAT I NEED WHEN I PRAY

Do not worry. Learn to pray about everything.
Give thanks to God as you ask Him for what you need.
PHILIPPIANS 4:6

Dear God, when I pray, I know that I can ask You for whatever I need. I can ask for big things, like help with my problems, and I can ask You for little things too. I understand that sometimes You won't give me exactly what I have asked for. That is because You know better what I need and when I need it. Thank You for always giving me Your best. Good night, God. Amen.

THINK ABOUT IT!

Is anything ever too big for God to handle?

GOD HEARS MY PRAYERS

"Then you will call upon Me and come and pray to Me, and I will listen to you."

JEREMIAH 29:12

Dear God, You made a promise to hear my prayers. I like that promise! You hear every word I say. You are never too busy to hear me. Whether I say something simple, like "Good morning, God" or "Good night," You hear my words. You hear me when I tell You my feelings, when I ask for Your help, or when I just want to talk with You. Thank You for hearing me, God. Amen.

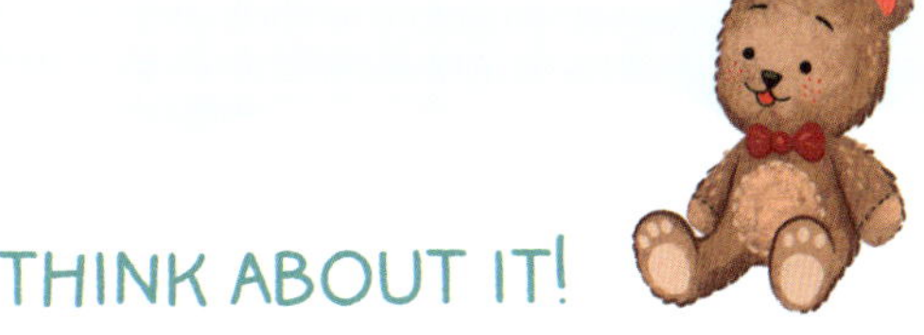

THINK ABOUT IT!

Is God ever too busy to listen to you?

GOD LISTENS TO ME

My God will hear me.

MICAH 7:7

Dear God, You don't just hear my prayers; You know my voice, and You care what I say. You think about my words. You listen to all my prayers with love. That makes me feel good. You are the very best listener because You always take time to hear me. Please help me to remember that I can pray anytime, anywhere, and You will listen and care about what I say. Thank You for listening tonight. Amen.

THINK ABOUT IT!

How many good listeners do you know?

THE BIBLE IS GOD'S WORD

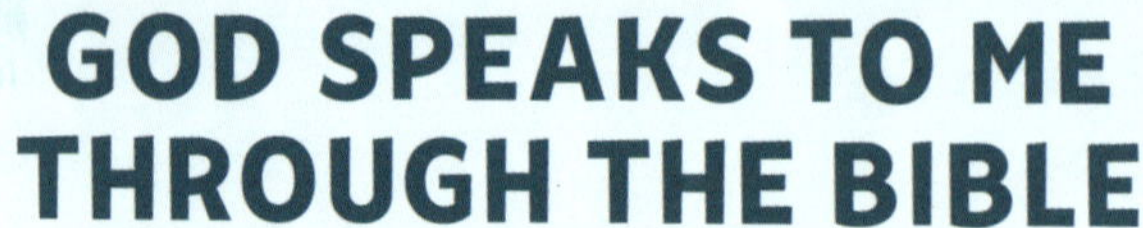

GOD SPEAKS TO ME THROUGH THE BIBLE

All the Holy Writings are God-given and are made alive by Him. Man is helped when he is taught God's Word. It shows what is wrong. It changes the way of a man's life. It shows him how to be right with God.

2 TIMOTHY 3:16

Dear God, the Bible is a way that You speak to my heart. Your words in the Bible are for everyone. They help us and teach us right from wrong. The Bible will show me how to please You by living the right way. I'm glad that You gave us the Bible! Please lead me to people who will help me to learn and understand its words. Amen.

THINK ABOUT IT!

What is your favorite Bible verse and why?

THE BIBLE IS FOR TODAY

God's Word is living and powerful.

HEBREWS 4:12

Dear God, You promised that the words in the Bible are forever. You planned Your words for everyone who would read them. The Bible is for me today, and it is important to know what is in it. I know that I can learn from the Bible about my own life. Your words in the Bible will guide me every day, if I learn and follow them. Help me to do that, God. Amen.

How can the Bible help you in everyday life?

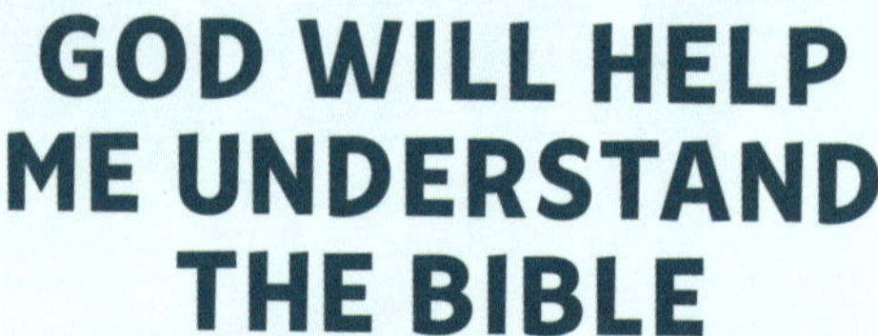

GOD WILL HELP ME UNDERSTAND THE BIBLE

Then He opened their minds to understand the Holy Writings.

LUKE 24:45

Dear God, some things about You are difficult to understand. You know that, so You gave us the Bible. You promised to help us understand You better through its stories and words. I want to learn more about You and how I can please You. If there is something in the Bible that I don't understand, remind me that I can ask someone to help me. Best of all, I can ask You! Thank You, God. Amen.

THINK ABOUT IT!

What is your favorite Bible story and why?

THE BIBLE WILL LEAD ME

Your Word is a lamp to my feet and a light to my path.

PSALM 119:105

Dear God, You said that the Bible is like a lamp. When I can't decide what to do, the Bible's words will help me to see—like a light does in the darkness. As I learn more about what is in the Bible, then I will know what to do when a problem comes my way. Will You help me with that, Father? I want the Bible to be like a bright light that leads me. Amen.

THINK ABOUT IT!

How can you shine your light for Jesus in the world?

THE BIBLE MAKES ME STRONG

Give me strength because of Your Word.

PSALM 119:28

Dear God, many of the Bible's stories are about people counting on You when they are troubled. I want to know and remember those stories. Everybody gets worried sometimes. When I do, I know that I can count on You and Your words in the Bible to help me. God, please speak to me through the Bible. Give me some words to remember—words that will help me to be strong whenever anything troubles me. Amen.

THINK ABOUT IT!

What helps you most when you are worried?

FAMILY, FRIENDS, AND NEIGHBORS

GOD PROVIDES A HOME FOR ME

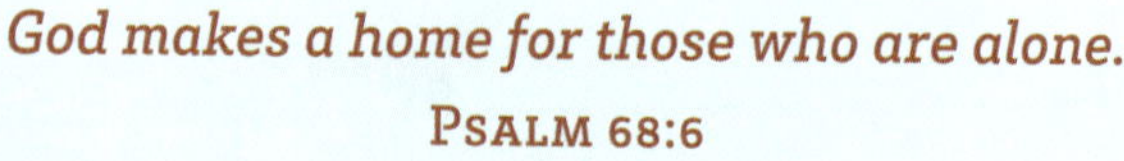

God makes a home for those who are alone.

PSALM 68:6

Dear God, thank You for giving me a home, and thank You for my family. There are some people who are lonely and homeless tonight. But You promised to make a home for everyone. Will You remind all the lonely and homeless people that You love them? I believe that You have a special place somewhere ready and waiting for them. Lead them there, please. Put them in a family who loves You. Amen.

THINK ABOUT IT!

What is your favorite thing about home?

GOD IS PLEASED WHEN I OBEY MY PARENTS

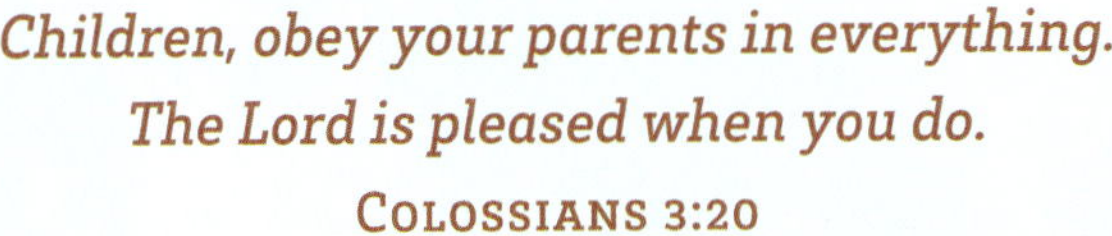

Children, obey your parents in everything.
The Lord is pleased when you do.
COLOSSIANS 3:20

Dear heavenly Father, I know that You forgive me when I mess up and don't obey my parents. They forgive me too. I want to get better at obeying and following their rules. Will You help me with that? Help me to listen to their words and do what they say. Remind me that my parents are Your helpers. When I obey them, it pleases You, and that makes all of us happy. Thank You, God. Amen.

THINK ABOUT IT!

Is it sometimes hard to obey your mom or dad? Why or why not?

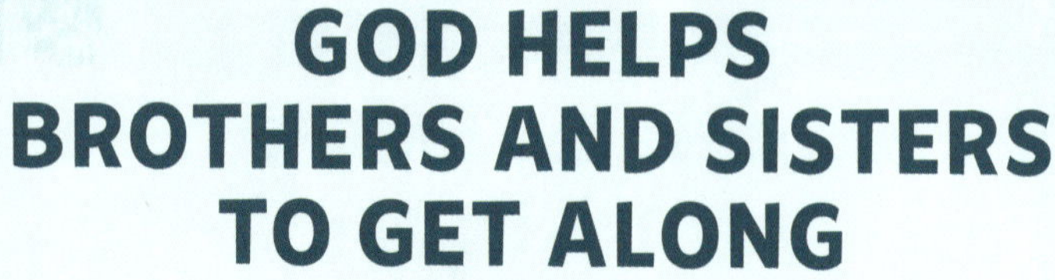

GOD HELPS BROTHERS AND SISTERS TO GET ALONG

See, how good and how pleasing it is for brothers to live together as one!

PSALM 133:1

Dear God, it makes You happy when brothers and sisters get along. You want us to love and help each other and share our toys. You expect us to be kind to one another and speak gently. It's hard for sisters and brothers to get along all the time! But, God, we have You to help us. Remind us of Your words, and help us to act in ways that are pleasing to You. Amen.

THINK ABOUT IT!

How does God want you to treat your family members?

GOD HELPS ME TO MAKE FRIENDS

He who stays away from others cares only about himself. He argues against all good wisdom.

PROVERBS 18:1

Dear God, thank You for friends. I want to have lots of friends so I can share You with them. I want to welcome new friends into my life all the time. Jesus is a friend to everyone. I want to be like Him. Maybe there is a kid in my neighborhood or at school who needs a friend. Will You get us together, God? Teach me to make friends and to be a good friend. Amen.

THINK ABOUT IT!

Who are your very best friends and why?

GOD TEACHES ME TO LOVE OTHERS

God has taught you to love each other.

1 THESSALONIANS 4:9

Dear God, You love me all the time. I want to love people like You do. You have promised to teach me how to love others. So help me, please, to learn from You and from the Bible how to be more loving. Jesus is my very best teacher. As I learn more about Him, I know that I will learn how to love my friends and my enemies. Teach me, dear God. Thank You. Amen.

THINK ABOUT IT!

Is it really possible to love your enemies?

GOD AND ME

GOD LOVES ME

I pray that you will be able to understand how wide and how long and how high and how deep His love is.

EPHESIANS 3:18

Dear God, will You help me to understand how big Your love is? The Bible says that Your love for me is greater than any other love. There are people here on earth who love me with all their hearts. But You love me even more! Your love for me is higher than the sky and deeper than the ocean. It makes me feel special that You love me so much. I love You too. Amen.

THINK ABOUT IT!

Does God love you more than anyone else on earth does?

NOTHING CAN SEPARATE ME FROM GOD'S LOVE

For I know that nothing can keep us from the love of God. Death cannot! Life cannot! Angels cannot! Leaders cannot! Any other power cannot! Hard things now or in the future cannot!

ROMANS 8:38

Dear God, if I don't feel Your love all around me, please remind me that it is still there. You rule heaven and earth, and You promised that nothing can separate me from Your love. No one is more powerful than You. You are the great King of everything, and no one can take Your love away from me. When I close my eyes to sleep tonight, please wrap me snugly in Your love. Amen.

THINK ABOUT IT!

Can anything get in the way of God's amazing love?

GOD SEES ME

The eyes of the Lord are on those who do what is right and good. His ears are open to their cry.

PSALM 34:15

Dear Father, I can't see You, but You see me. You especially like seeing when I do things that are right and good. And when I need Your help, You see that too. Thank You for keeping Your eyes on me, God. Wherever I go and whatever I do, I know that You see me. You hear my prayers, and You know exactly what I need. I will never be alone, because You are with me. Amen.

THINK ABOUT IT!

Are you ever really alone? Why or why not?

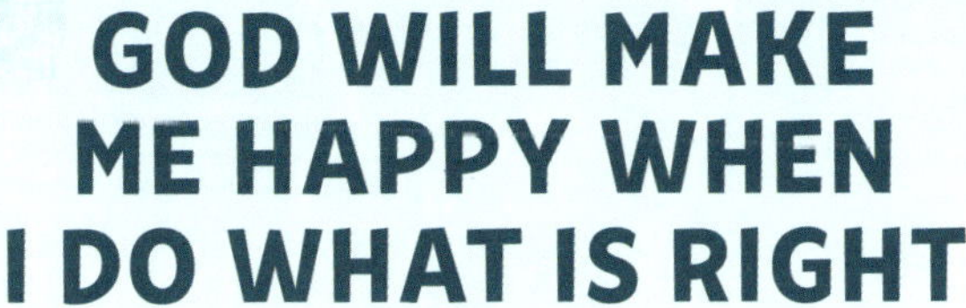

GOD WILL MAKE ME HAPPY WHEN I DO WHAT IS RIGHT

You meet him who finds joy in doing what is right and good, who remembers You in Your ways.

ISAIAH 64:5

Dear God, thank You for filling me up with glad feelings. When I do what is right, I feel peaceful in my heart, and when I do what is good, I feel happy. You are the one who teaches me how to be right and good. As I learn from You and try my best to be like You, I feel close to You, and that is the best feeling of all. Good night, God. Amen.

THINK ABOUT IT!

When do you feel closest to God?

I CAN DO GREAT THINGS WITH GOD'S HELP

God is able to do much more than we ask or think through His power working in us.

EPHESIANS 3:20

Dear God, I wonder what I will be when I grow up. You promised that I can do much more than I think I can because Your power is at work inside me. Lead me to give my best to everything I do. Remind me that You have a great plan for my future. I will always be Your helper here on earth. Teach me and help me to learn so we can do great things together! Amen.

THINK ABOUT IT!

Why is it important to always give your best effort in everything you do?

DEAR GOD, I TRUST YOU

TRUSTING GOD MAKES ME STRONG

Those who trust in the Lord are like Mount Zion, which cannot be moved but stands forever.

PSALM 125:1

Dear God, You promised that if I trust You, I can stand up to anything that gets in my way. You are the Father of all fathers. You have power over everything, and You always know the right thing to do. I know that I can trust You to help me all the time. So please build up my trust in You. Make it big and strong. Help me to trust You with everything I do. Amen.

THINK ABOUT IT!

Is it easy for you to stand up to things that get in the way of your relationship with God? Why or why not?

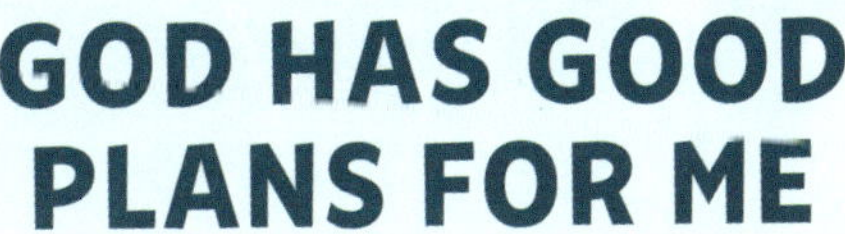

GOD HAS GOOD PLANS FOR ME

" 'For I know the plans I have for you,' says the Lord, 'plans for well-being and not for trouble, to give you a future and a hope.' "

JEREMIAH 29:11

Dear God, I wish that I knew what Your plans are for me. But for now, that is Your secret. You promise that Your plans for me are good. You want me to have a good life. That is all I can know right now about my future. I need to trust You with the rest. I do trust You, God. I believe that You have great things planned for me because You love me. Amen.

THINK ABOUT IT!

What plans do you think God might have for your life?

GOD WILL ALWAYS HELP ME

*Let us go with complete trust to the throne of God.
We will receive His loving-kindness and have
His loving-favor to help us whenever we need it.*

HEBREWS 4:16

Dear God, sometimes I like to imagine You as the great King sitting on Your throne in heaven. You are a King who welcomes people in. We can come to You at any time, night or day, to pray and ask for Your help. Best of all, we can trust You to listen to us and help us. God, I am so glad that You are my King! Thank You. I love You. Amen.

THINK ABOUT IT!

What kind of King is God?

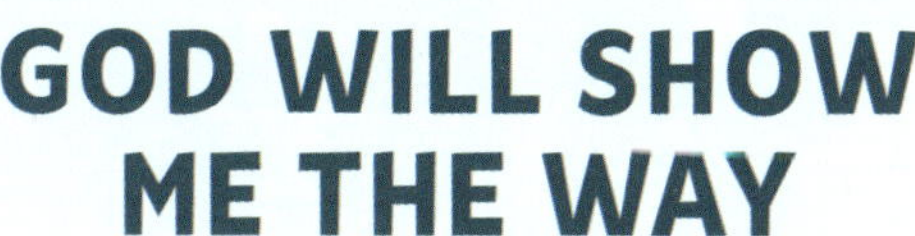

GOD WILL SHOW ME THE WAY

Teach me the way I should go
for I lift up my soul to You.
PSALM 143:8

Dear God, I feel safe knowing that You are always with me. If I have to go someplace I have never been before, I don't have to worry because You know the way to get there. If I don't know how to do something, You know how to get it done. All I have to do is trust You to show me the way. Please teach me to trust You even more. Thank You, God. Amen.

THINK ABOUT IT!

How does God's Word show you the right way to go?

JESUS IS ALWAYS NEAR ME

Come close to God and He will come close to you.

JAMES 4:8

Dear Jesus, when I put all my trust in You, I feel closer to You. It is like I am resting in Your arms, and You are rocking me to sleep. I feel safe and sound knowing that You are near to me. Help me to remember that You are always with me and that You love me. All I have to do is say Your name, Jesus, and know that You are here. Amen.

THINK ABOUT IT!

Do you trust God with all your heart? Why or why not?

GOD IS MINE FOREVER

THERE IS ONLY ONE GOD

"I am the Lord, and there is no other. There is no God besides Me."

ISAIAH 45:5

Dear God, I believe with all my heart that You are the one and only God. Nothing is bigger, stronger, or better than You, and still You are never too busy for a kid like me. I love that about You. You always have time for me. You stay with me day and night, watch over me, and help me. Oh God, I love You so much! Thank You for being my heavenly Father forever. Amen.

THINK ABOUT IT!

Do you believe with all your heart that God is the one true God?

GOD'S PROMISES ARE FOREVER

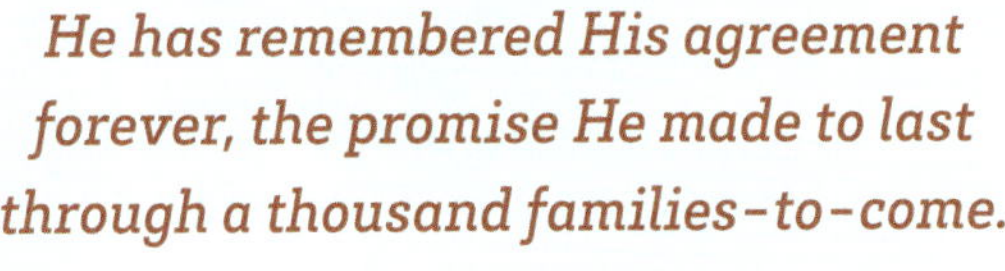

He has remembered His agreement forever, the promise He made to last through a thousand families-to-come.

PSALM 105:8

Dear God, thank You for teaching me about Your promises. Please help me to remember them and trust in them every day. Remind me that Your promises are forever. You will never change them or break them. I want to share with my family and friends what I have learned about You. Will You teach me how to do that? I want everyone to know how wonderful You are. I love You, God. Amen.

THINK ABOUT IT!

Do you think it's hard to keep promises? Why or why not?

GOD WILL NEVER LEAVE ME

Those who know Your name will put their trust in You. For You, O Lord, have never left alone those who look for You.

PSALM 9:10

Heavenly Father, one of the best promises is that You will stay with me forever. You made me, and You have been with me every minute of my life. As I grow up, You will be with me all the time. Even when I am very old, You will still be here, loving me and helping me. Please fill up my heart with love for You, and help me to love You more each day. Amen.

THINK ABOUT IT!

What is your favorite Bible promise?

JESUS IS MY SAVIOR

We have seen and are able to say that the Father sent His Son to save the world from the punishment of sin.

1 JOHN 4:14

Dear Jesus, God's Son, You came to save the world from sin. You love me, and You are the best example of how God wants me to live. As I grow up, I want to learn to be more like You. Come into my heart and teach me, Jesus. I know that You are my best friend forever. You are always with me. I will talk to You and trust You to help me. Amen.

THINK ABOUT IT!

Why did God send Jesus into the world?

GOD'S PROMISES ARE PERFECT AND GREAT

Through His shining-greatness and perfect life, He has given us promises. These promises are of great worth and no amount of money can buy them.

2 PETER 1:4

Dear God, it's time to say good night. But, before I sleep, I want to thank You for sharing Your promises with me. Help me to remember them all. Every day, please teach me more about You, and every night remind me that I am special because I am Yours. Your promises are perfect and great. Your love for me fills up my heart. I love You too, God, now and forever. Good night, and thank You. Amen.

THINK ABOUT IT!

What was the best thing about your day?